# BORING BIBLE

## INSTANT LESSON MATERIAL

### THE BOOK OF ACTS

### ANDY ROBB

**kevin mayhew**

First published in 2004 by

KEVIN MAYHEW LTD

Buxhall, Stowmarket, Suffolk, IP14 3BW

E-mail: info@kevinmayhewltd.com

KINGSGATE PUBLISHING INC

1000 Pannell Street, Suite G, Columbia, MO 65201

E-mail: sales@kingsgatepublishing.com

9 8 7 6 5 4 3 2 1 0

ISBN 1 84417 248 1

Catalogue No 1500701

Cover illustration by Andy Robb

Cover design by Angela Selfe

Typesetting by Andy Robb

Printed and bound in Great Britain

# CONTENTS

# HOW TO USE THIS BOOK

As far as most kids are concerned, the Bible is probably the most mind-numbingly boring book they could think of.

But what's even more surprising is that most of them have never even read the teensiest snatch of the book.

In fact, most kids wouldn't know their Gideon from their Goliath if it hit them right between the eyes! (Sorry about the analogy.)

So, when it comes to teaching them a thing or two about some of the stuff that's in the Bible then you're probably better off giving them the option of revising for a maths test or going to the opera.

Let's face it – for most kids the Bible is just one big turn-off, which is a shame because it's the one book that's going to help them make some sort of sense of their young lives.

So if you happen to be landed with (I mean have the privilege of) unpacking the Bible to kids then the task set before you can seem like an uphill struggle.

**Fear not!**

That's where this **Boring Bible Instant Lesson Material** book comes in.

This book provides you with a fresh and a fun way to bring to life familiar (or perhaps hard to understand) Bible stories in a handy, ready-to-use format and in a way that will appeal to kids.

Each book contains **25 Bible stories** to choose from and features a snapshot of the background to each Bible passage selected, the key characters involved and Bible passage reproduced in its entirety.

All this appears on the left-hand side of each double page spread which is purely for your consumption.

On the facing page is the material that's designed totally with the kids in mind and retells the Bible passage in the inimitable Boring Bible style. (High on humour – low on waffle.)

So, now that you've parted with money for this product, how exactly do you use it?

# SOME SERVING SUGGESTIONS

Because the situations and circumstances of every purchaser of this product vary, there are no hard and fast rules as to how to make the most of the **Boring Bible Instant Lesson Material**.

You may, for instance, be covering one or more of the featured Bible stories in a school setting.

Alternatively, you may be a Sunday school teacher.

The material in this book might aid you to deliver a complete Bible teaching session or perhaps simply to enhance or supplement something you've already prepared.

Either way, this book should make your task easier – and more fun!

**Here are some suggestions:**

- Give the kids a quick overview of the Bible passage you've selected (as explained in the teacher's page), read them the Bible passage and then hand out photocopies of the kids' page for them to read on their own.

  If you've got time to spare, how about allowing them to colour in the cartoon picture?

- Explain the background to the Bible story, hand out photocopies of the kids' page and then you read it out while they follow it.

  You could even put the cartoon picture on an OHP to display at the relevant point in the story.

- Perhaps you're doing an upfront kids' talk at church and need to retell a Bible passage in a way that engages the kids.

  Why not use the kids' page as your script and pop the cartoon picture on to an OHP?

- Or if you've been teaching on one of the featured Bible passages in this book then why not use the kids' page as a take-home sheet to act as a handy reminder of what they've learned.

No doubt you'll find other creative ways to use this product but the bottom line is that it's here to make your job easier and for the kids to have a clearer understanding of what the Bible is about and what it has to say to them.

Have fun!

# PENTECOST

**WHAT'S IT ALL ABOUT?**

This Bible story is all about how God's Holy Spirit kick-started Jesus' church

**WHO ARE THE MAIN CHARACTERS?**

A bunch of believers (who included Peter), some scathing Jews and of course, the Holy Spirit

**WHERE'S IT FOUND IN THE BIBLE?**

Acts 2:1-19

**HERE'S THE BIBLE PASSAGE...**

When the day of Pentecost came, all the believers were gathered together in one place. Suddenly there was a noise from the sky which sounded like a strong wind blowing, and it filled the whole house where they were sitting. Then they saw what looked like tongues of fire which spread out and touched each person there.

They were all filled with the Holy Spirit and began to talk in other languages, as the Spirit enabled them to speak.

There were Jews living in Jerusalem, religious people who had come from every country in the world. When they heard this noise, a large crowd gathered.

They were all excited, because each one of them heard the believers speaking in his or her own language.

In amazement and wonder they exclaimed, 'These people who are talking like this are Galileans! How is it, then, that all of us hear them speaking in our own native languages? We are from Parthia, Media, and Elam; from Mesopotamia, Judea, and Cappadocia; from Pontus and Asia, from Phrygia and Pamphylia, from Egypt and the regions of Libya near Cyrene. Some of us are from Rome, both Jews and Gentiles converted to Judaism, and some of us are from Crete and Arabia – yet all of us hear them speaking in our own languages about the great things that God has done!'

Amazed and confused, they kept asking each other, 'What does this mean?'

But others made fun of the believers, saying, 'These people are drunk!'

Then Peter stood up with the other eleven apostles and in a loud voice began to speak to the crowd: 'Fellow-Jews and all of you who live in Jerusalem, listen to me and let me tell you what this means. These people are not drunk, as you suppose; it is only nine o'clock in the morning.

'Instead, this is what the prophet Joel spoke about: "This is what I will do in the last days, God says: I will pour out my Spirit on everyone.

'"Your sons and daughters will proclaim my message; your young men will see visions, and your old men will have dreams.

'"Yes, even on my servants, both men and women, I will pour out my Spirit in those days, and they will proclaim my message.

'"I will perform miracles in the sky above and wonders on the earth below."'

# POWER SHOWER!

If you know *anything* about Jesus and the Bible then the chances are you've heard of a bunch of guys called **'the disciples'**. They were the men who **Jesus** trained up to carry on his work (of telling people that God loved them and wanted to be their friend) after Jesus had died and gone back to heaven.

But just *before* he left them, Jesus told his disciples to hang around in **Jerusalem** and wait. Wait for what? I'll tell you. One of the secrets of Jesus' success was that he was chock-a-block full of **God's Holy Spirit**.

*That's* how Jesus was able to do all those amazing miracles like **healing people** and bringing people back from the **dead**. If the disciples were gonna do the *same* sort of stuff *as Jesus* then they were *also* gonna need a mega fill-up with the Holy Spirit.

And that's where we catch up with these guys in *this* Bible bit. Holed up in a house somewhere in Jerusalem (along with loads of other followers of Jesus) they waited . . . and waited . . . and waited. Then suddenly, with a **whoosh like the wind**, and looking like **tongues of fire**, the Holy Spirit turned up . . . **big time!** Everyone in the place was filled with the Holy Spirit but what happened next was even *more* amazing.

Jesus' followers all started to speak . . . but in **different languages**. These weren't languages they'd quickly learnt at evening classes. These were special languages and words that the Holy Spirit was now giving them to speak. It was such a din that passers-by wondered what on earth was going on . . .

But **Peter** soon silenced them. Full of God's power, Peter put them straight by telling all and sundry that what they were witnessing was exactly what God had promised long, long ago.

What *had* God promised?

God had promised that one day he would send his Holy Spirit on young and old alike so that with God's power inside of them they could change the world from bad to good.

They weren't drunk – they were just **supercharged followers of Jesus** who couldn't shut up about how Jesus had changed their lives.

And just in case you were wondering *what* languages the disciples (and co.) were speaking, let me tell you that they were the very *same* languages that those passers-by spoke. Jerusalem was packed out with visitors from far and wide who'd come to celebrate the festival of **Pentecost**.

They'd heard all about Jesus (and how he can change your life) in their **own language** so when they went home (after the Pentecost knees-up was over) that message about Jesus was gonna go back with them.

Now that's what I *call* a smart piece of **advertising** on God's part!

# A LAME MAN GETS HEALED

## WHAT'S IT ALL ABOUT?

This Bible story is about the dynamic first steps of Jesus' fledgling church

## WHO ARE THE MAIN CHARACTERS?

Peter, John and a lame man. (Not forgetting the entire church community along with its apostles)

## WHERE'S IT FOUND IN THE BIBLE?

Acts 2:43- 47 and 3:1-10

## HERE'S THE BIBLE PASSAGE...

Many miracles and wonders were being done through the apostles, and everyone was filled with awe.

All the believers continued together in close fellowship and shared their belongings with one another. They would sell their property and possessions, and distribute the money among all, according to what each one needed.

Day after day they met as a group in the Temple, and they had their meals together in their homes, eating with glad and humble hearts, praising God, and enjoying the good will of all the people. And every day the Lord added to their group those who were being saved. One day Peter and John went to the Temple at three o'clock in the afternoon, the hour for prayer.

There at the Beautiful Gate, as it was called, was a man who had been lame all his life.

Every day he was carried to the gate to beg for money from the people who were going into the Temple. When he saw Peter and John going in, he begged them to give him something.

They looked straight at him, and Peter said, 'Look at us!' So he looked at them, expecting to get something from them.

But Peter said to him, 'I have no money at all, but I give you what I have: in the name of Jesus Christ of Nazareth I order you to get up and walk!' Then he took him by his right hand and helped him up.

At once the man's feet and ankles became strong; he jumped up, stood on his feet, and started walking around. Then he went into the Temple with them, walking and jumping and praising God.

The people there saw him walking and praising God, and when they recognised him as the beggar who had sat at the Beautiful Gate, they were all surprised and amazed at what had happened to him.

# MIRACLE MAN!

*This* Bible story is all about the early days of the **world's first church** (3,000 members and growing fast!). With the Holy Spirit living inside of them, miracles were happening thick and fast.

Not only that but you just couldn't seem to stop these followers of Jesus from being **generous**. Everyone was sharing their possessions with each other so that *nobody* went without. Jesus had done so much for them that they wanted to pass it on.

One day, **Peter** (one of their leaders) and **John** were headed for the Temple where the church had taken to holding its meetings.

*Outside* the Temple, at a place called the **Beautiful Gate** (as the Bible handily informs us) was a beggar called . . . well, we don't actually *know* his name but what we *do* know is that he was **lame** (which means he couldn't walk – but then you probably knew that already, didn't you?).

Not one to pass up an opportunity to relieve someone of their hard-earned cash, the beggar stopped Peter and John in their tracks and asked for money.

The pair of them had probably been a bit *over*-generous with sharing their possessions 'cos this was Peter's reply . . .

And guess what? Our penniless pair hoisted the man to his feet and the lame man's ankles instantly became strong. He could walk! It was a **miracle**!

Job done, Peter and John made their merry way to the Temple, no doubt to join the rest of the church who were busily praising God. The Bible says that the miracle man followed hot on their heels (well, perhaps not *quite* in those words).

When regulars to the Temple saw the lame man (or should I say *ex*-lame man?) they were bowled over by what God had done.

I don't know about you but I reckon that the beggar probably became the church's newest member that very day, don't you?

# ANANIAS AND SAPPHIRA

## WHAT'S IT ALL ABOUT?

This Bible story is about how Ananias and Sapphira cheated on God and the high price they paid for their greed

## WHO ARE THE MAIN CHARACTERS?

Husband and wife team, Ananias and Sapphira star with Peter and the corpse carriers as extras

## WHERE'S IT FOUND IN THE BIBLE?

Acts 4:32-37 and 5:1-11

## HERE'S THE BIBLE PASSAGE...

The group of believers was one in mind and heart. None of them said that any of their belongings were their own, but they all shared with one another everything they had.

With great power the apostles gave witness to the resurrection of the Lord Jesus, and God poured rich blessings on them all.

There was no one in the group who was in need. Those who owned fields or houses would sell them, bring the money received from the sale, and hand it over to the apostles; and the money was distributed to each one according to his need.

And so it was that Joseph, a Levite born in Cyprus, whom the apostles called Barnabas (which means 'One who Encourages'), sold a field he owned, brought the money, and handed it over to the apostles. But there was a man named Ananias, who with his wife Sapphira sold some property that belonged to them. But with his wife's agreement he kept part of the money for himself and handed the rest over to the apostles.

Peter said to him, 'Ananias, why did you let Satan take control of you and make you lie to the Holy Spirit by keeping part of the money you received for the property? Before you sold the property, it belonged to you; and after you sold it, the money was yours. Why, then, did you decide to do such a thing?

'You have not lied to human beings – you have lied to God!' As soon as Ananias heard this, he fell down dead; and all who heard about it were terrified.

The young men came in, wrapped up his body, carried him out, and buried him.

About three hours later his wife, not knowing what had happened, came in.

Peter asked her, 'Tell me, was this the full amount you and your husband received for your property?'

'Yes,' she answered, 'the full amount.'

So Peter said to her, 'Why did you and your husband decide to put the Lord's Spirit to the test? The men who buried your husband are now at the door, and they will carry you out too!'

At once she fell down at his feet and died. The young men came in and saw that she was dead, so they carried her out and buried her beside her husband.

The whole church and all the others who heard of this were terrified.

# DOUBLE DOUBLE-CROSSERS!

Right from square one, Jesus' church got itself a bit of a reputation for being **selfless** (which is another way of saying the people were 'unselfish'). Sharing their possessions was becoming the norm.

But it didn't stop *there*. No way!

People were selling their **houses** and **land** as *well* and then handing it over to the church leaders (called **apostles**) so that they could share it round to the poor and needy.

The Bible says that a guy called **Joseph** sold a field (which *he* owned, obviously) and gave the proceeds to the apostles to do their stuff with.

Next up, **Ananias** and **Sapphira** (a hubbie and his wife) decided that *they'd* like to follow in Joseph's footsteps and flog a bit of property of *theirs*.

Which is precisely what they did – with one difference. The scheming pair kept *back* some of the dosh (from the sale of the property) for *themselves*. As you'll soon find out, banking some of the money for themselves *wasn't* a very good move.

What Ananias *hadn't* banked on was the Holy Spirit filling in **Peter** (the main apostle) with their sneaky plan.

ANANIAS... WHY DID YOU LIE TO THE HOLY SPIRIT BY KEEPING PART OF THE MONEY YOU RECEIVED FOR THE PROPERTY?

Peter didn't wait for an answer. He pointed out (loud and clear) that Ananias had lied to the Holy Spirit (God) and with that . . . Ananias **dropped down dead**!

Peter had Ananias's body carted away by some of the young men to make the place ready for a visit from the other half of the **deceiving duo**. Sure enough, three hours later, Sapphira burst in wanting to know where her hubbie was.

Peter didn't have time for a cosy chit-chat. Instead he launched headlong into quizzing Sapphira as to whether this was the full amount of cash – or not?

I suppose that she *could* have come clean and told the truth, but Sapphira just dug herself in **deeper**. **'The full amount'**, was her reply. And no prizes for guessing what became of Ananias's wife?

Yep, she dropped down stone dead as well. Bring on the young men again. There's *another* body that needs carting away .

I'll tell you something *else*. What happened to Ananias and Sapphira really scared the pants off the whole church. *One* thing's for sure, I'll bet that nobody dared lie to God again!

# APOSTLES PERSECUTED

## WHAT'S IT ALL ABOUT?

This Bible story is about how the jealous religious leaders had the apostles locked up – only for an angel to release them again

## WHO ARE THE MAIN CHARACTERS?

Various religious leaders, various apostles and various red-faced prison guards

## WHERE'S IT FOUND IN THE BIBLE?

Acts 5:12-25

## HERE'S THE BIBLE PASSAGE...

Many miracles and wonders were being performed among the people by the apostles. All the believers met together in Solomon's Porch. Nobody outside the group dared to join them, even though the people spoke highly of them. But more and more people were added to the group - a crowd of men and women who believed in the Lord. As a result of what the apostles were doing, sick people were carried out into the streets and placed on beds and mats so that at least Peter's shadow might fall on some of them as he passed by.

And crowds of people came in from the towns around Jerusalem, bringing those who were ill or who had evil spirits in them; and they were all healed. Then the High Priest and all his companions, members of the local party of the Sadducees, became extremely jealous of the apostles; so they decided to take action.

They arrested the apostles and put them in the public jail. But that night an angel of the Lord opened the prison gates, led the apostles out, and said to them, 'Go and stand in the Temple, and tell the people all about this new life.' The apostles obeyed, and at dawn they entered the Temple and started teaching.

The High Priest and his companions called together all the Jewish elders for a full meeting of the Council; then they sent orders to the prison to have the apostles brought before them. But when the officials arrived, they did not find the apostles in prison, so they returned to the Council and reported, 'When we arrived at the jail, we found it locked up tight and all the guards on watch at the gates; but when we opened the gates, we found no one inside!'

When the chief priests and the officer in charge of the Temple guards heard this, they wondered what had happened to the apostles. Then a man came in and said to them, 'Listen! The men you put in prison are in the Temple teaching the people!'

# JAILBREAK!

If you'd happened to live in **Jerusalem** around the early part of the first century AD then you couldn't have failed to notice that something rather unusual was going on.

People were getting healed of all sorts of **nasty sicknesses** and **diseases** and it was all thanks to the local church. In fact, if you asked the *church* they'd tell you that it was all thanks to *Jesus*, 'cos it was *his* church. So credit where credit's due, eh?

Anyway, as it was, sick people were coming from far and wide in the hope of getting as near as they could to the **apostles** (that's the church's leaders) who were carrying out all these miracles (on Jesus' behalf). Not *everybody* was thrilled about what was happening.

The Jewish **religious leaders** were green with envy that these apostles seemed to be getting the lion's share of the attention from the crowds . . . instead of *them*. So they decided to put a stop to it. First off they had the apostles arrested and chucked in jail.

Don't get *too* upset 'cos help is already on its way. God dispatched an **angel** to pay a surprise visit to the apostles. Ignoring the fact that they were locked in, the angel opened the prison gates and led them all to freedom – without the prison guards even suspecting a thing! Now that's what I *call* clever.

Once they were outside the angel told the apostles to go back to the Temple (where they'd been arrested) and continue to tell people about Jesus.

Meantime, the religious leaders had hit upon the idea of cross-examining the apostles to see what they had to say for themselves. Little did they know what had been going on behind their backs. When the prison guards went to fetch the apostles, all they found was an **empty cell**.

The religious leaders were none too pleased when they realised that they'd been well and truly **out-smarted** and that the apostles were back at the Temple doing their stuff **as bold as brass**.

# STEPHEN IS KILLED

**WHAT'S IT ALL ABOUT?**

This Bible story is all about the first person to be killed for being a follower of Jesus

**WHO ARE THE MAIN CHARACTERS?**

Stephen, a whole host of Jewish big-wigs and Saul (cloak-care dept.)

**WHERE'S IT FOUND IN THE BIBLE?**

Acts 6:8-15, 7:51-60 and 8:1-3

**HERE'S THE BIBLE PASSAGE...**

Stephen, a man richly blessed by God and full of power, performed great miracles and wonders among the people. But he was opposed by some men who were members of the synagogue of the Freedmen (as it was called), which included Jews from Cyrene and Alexandria.

They and other Jews from the provinces of Cilicia and Asia started arguing with Stephen. But the Spirit gave Stephen such wisdom that when he spoke, they could not refute him. So they bribed some men to say, 'We heard him speaking against Moses and against God!' In this way they stirred up the people, the elders, and the teachers of the Law.

They seized Stephen and took him before the Council. Then they brought in some men to tell lies about him. 'This man,' they said, 'is always talking against our sacred Temple and the Law of Moses. We heard him say that this Jesus of Nazareth will tear down the Temple and change all the customs which have come down to us from Moses!'

All those sitting in the Council fixed their eyes on Stephen and saw that his face looked like the face of an angel. 'How stubborn you are!' Stephen went on to say. 'How heathen your hearts, how deaf you are to God's message! You are just like your ancestors: you too have always resisted the Holy Spirit! Was there any prophet that your ancestors did not persecute?

'They killed God's messengers, who long ago announced the coming of his righteous Servant. And now you have betrayed and murdered him.

'You are the ones who received God's law, that was handed down by angels – yet you have not obeyed it!' As the members of the Council listened to Stephen, they became furious and ground their teeth at him in anger.

But Stephen, full of the Holy Spirit, looked up to heaven and saw God's glory and Jesus standing at the right-hand side of God. 'Look!' he said. 'I see heaven opened and the Son of Man standing at the right-hand side of God!'

With a loud cry the members of the Council covered their ears with their hands.

Then they all rushed at him at once, threw him out of the city, and stoned him. The witnesses left their cloaks in the care of a young man named Saul.

They kept on stoning Stephen as he called out to the Lord, 'Lord Jesus, receive my spirit!' He knelt down and cried out in a loud voice, 'Lord! Do not remember this sin against them!' He said this and died.

But Saul tried to destroy the church; going from house to house, he dragged out the believers, both men and women, and threw them into jail.

# STONE DEAD!

For *this* Bible story we're headed for **Jerusalem** (the capital city of Israel) where trouble is a-brewing for a bunch of guys (*and* gals) who'd jacked in living lives *their* way and had decided to live life *God's* way.

They were all followers of **Jesus** (God's Son who'd recently been executed but had come back to life again) and *they* were now getting picked on for the same reasons that people picked on *Jesus*. And what reason was that? Simple. People didn't like being told what to do – expecially when it was *God* who was doing the telling.

The **religious leaders** were the *worst* culprits. They should have known better, after all it was *their* job to keep the Jewish people on track with God but *instead* they'd ended up sucking the life out of everything with their tedious lists of '**do's**' and '**don'ts**'.

When a fella called **Stephen** started doing all sorts of **amazing miracles** (using the power and authority that Jesus had given him) these religious leaders were *well* miffed. The religious leaders tried to have it out with Stephen but even though they argued with him 'til they were blue in the face they simply couldn't get one over on this **godly guy**.

(Jesus had given Stephen a mega dollop of **wisdom** which he used to out-smart them.) There was nothing for it but for these riled religious leaders to bribe a few willing crooks to accuse Stephen of saying something against their Law – which was exactly what happened.

Instead of getting hot under the collar about these **trumped-up charges** (like his accusers were) Stephen remained as **cool as a cucumber**. In fact (so the Bible tells us) Stephen's face looked like the **face of an angel**.

Once they'd all shut up, Stephen gave them all a **history refresher course** on who God *was* and what he'd *done* for the Jewish people. To be perfectly honest, the religious leaders weren't particularly in the mood for a lecture about how they'd failed God and when Stephen **put the boot in** by letting them know (loud and clear) that God held *them* responsible for murdering Jesus they were **teeth-gnashingly livid**.

The Bible even says that the religious leaders put their hands over their ears 'cos they didn't like what they were hearing. No surprise!

Grabbing Stephen by force, the angry mob dragged Stephen outside the city and **stoned him to death**. Would you believe it? Just before Stephen died he asked God to **forgive his killers**. Stephen wasn't troubled by his imminent death. Stephen already had his sights fixed on heaven where he was gonna be any moment now. But what about that fella (**Saul**) who was holding everyone's cloaks while Stephen was being stoned? I wonder what was running through *his* mind? Well, more of him later.

# SAMARIA RECEIVES JESUS

## WHAT'S IT ALL ABOUT?

This Bible story is about how Philip preaches the gospel to Samaria and a magician called Simon gets the wrong end of the stick

## WHO ARE THE MAIN CHARACTERS?

Philip, Simon (the magician), Peter and John, the people of Samaria

## WHERE'S IT FOUND IN THE BIBLE?

Acts 8:4-25

## HERE'S THE BIBLE PASSAGE...

The believers who were scattered went everywhere, preaching the message. Philip went to the principal city in Samaria and preached the Messiah to the people there.

The crowds paid close attention to what Philip said, as they listened to him and saw the miracles that he performed.

Evil spirits came out from many people with a loud cry, and many paralysed and lame people were healed. So there was great joy in that city.

A man named Simon lived there, who for some time had astounded the Samaritans with his magic. He claimed that he was someone great, and everyone in the city, from all classes of society, paid close attention to him.

'He is that power of God known as "The Great Power",' they said. They paid this attention to him because for such a long time he had astonished them with his magic.

But when they believed Philip's message about the good news of the Kingdom of God and about Jesus Christ, they were baptised, both men and women.

Simon himself also believed; and after being baptised, he stayed close to Philip and was astounded when he saw the great wonders and miracles that were being performed.

The apostles in Jerusalem heard that the people of Samaria had received the word of God, so they sent Peter and John to them. When they arrived, they prayed for the believers that they might receive the Holy Spirit.

For the Holy Spirit had not yet come down on any of them; they had only been baptised in the name of the Lord Jesus. Then Peter and John placed their hands on them, and they received the Holy Spirit.

Simon saw that the Spirit had been given to the believers when the apostles placed their hands on them.

So he offered money to Peter and John, and said, 'Give this power to me too, so that anyone I place my hands on will receive the Holy Spirit.'

But Peter answered him, 'May you and your money go to hell, for thinking that you can buy God's gift with money! You have no part or share in our work, because your heart is not right in God's sight.

'Repent, then, of this evil plan of yours, and pray to the Lord that he will forgive you for thinking such a thing as this. For I see that you are full of bitter envy and are a prisoner of sin.'

Simon said to Peter and John, 'Please pray to the Lord for me, so that none of these things you spoke of will happen to me.'

After they had given their testimony and proclaimed the Lord's message, Peter and John went back to Jerusalem.

On their way they preached the Good News in many villages of Samaria.

# SIMPLE SIMON!

Ever heard of the **early church**? (No, they *weren't* the people who got up at the **crack of dawn** to get a front row seat!) These were the people who made up **Jesus' church** when it had just got up and running. And there was just no *stopping* these guys.

We catch up with a chap called **Philip** in a place called **Samaria** where he's busily telling all-comers that *anyone* can become a friend of God 'cos Jesus has taken the punishment for their sin (which happened to be getting in the *way* of them being God's friend).

To back up his message, Philip healed *oodles* of people (in God's power) to prove that God was real and that God really *was* interested in caring for his creation. Miracles were nothing new to the city where Philip was doing his stuff.

A guy called **Simon** (a magician) had made a bit of a name for himself by doing all sorts of magic to impress the people. When this **minor magical celebrit**y saw the miracles *Philip* was performing he chucked away his magic wand and became a believer in Jesus – there and then!

But Simon was a bit slow on the uptake.

When a couple of Philip's mates from church (**Peter** and **John**) turned up and prayed for the new believers in Jesus (by laying their hands on them) to be filled with God's **Holy Spirit**, Simon put his foot in it **big time**!

Simon offered Peter and John some of his **hard-earned cash** in exchange for the ability to lay his hands on people so that they'd *also* get filled with the Holy Spirit.

Simon probably thought this was just another magic trick – but he couldn't have been *more* mistaken.

Peter told Simon (in no uncertain terms) where to put his money and that **he'd missed the point**. This Jesus stuff wasn't about making a name for yourself – it was about *Jesus* getting all the credit. Peter told Simon to sort himself out and get his motives right – maybe, just maybe, God could then use him.

# THE ETHIOPIAN OFFICIAL

## WHAT'S IT ALL ABOUT?

This Bible story is about when Philip outruns a carriage, heads up an on-board Bible study and then simply vanishes

## WHO ARE THE MAIN CHARACTERS?

Philip, an Ethiopian official and a rather comfy carriage

## WHERE'S IT FOUND IN THE BIBLE?

Acts 8:26-40

## HERE'S THE BIBLE PASSAGE...

An angel of the Lord said to Philip, 'Get ready and go south to the road that goes from Jerusalem to Gaza.' (This road is not used nowadays.)

So Philip got ready and went. Now an Ethiopian eunuch, who was an important official in charge of the treasury of the queen of Ethiopia, was on his way home. He had been to Jerusalem to worship God and was going back home in his carriage. As he rode along, he was reading from the book of the prophet Isaiah. The Holy Spirit said to Philip,

'Go over to that carriage and stay close to it.' Philip ran over and heard him reading from the book of the prophet Isaiah. He asked him, 'Do you understand what you are reading?'

The official replied, 'How can I understand unless someone explains it to me?' And he invited Philip to climb up and sit in the carriage with him. The passage of scripture which he was reading was this:

'Like a sheep that is taken to be slaughtered, like a lamb that makes no sound when its wool is cut off, he did not say a word. He was humiliated, and justice was denied him.

'No one will be able to tell about his descendants, because his life on earth has come to an end.' The official asked Philip, 'Tell me, of whom is the prophet saying this? Of himself or of someone else?' Then Philip began to speak; starting from this passage of scripture, he told him the Good News about Jesus.

As they travelled down the road, they came to a place where there was some water, and the official said, 'Here is some water. What is to keep me from being baptised?'

The official ordered the carriage to stop, and both Philip and the official went down into the water, and Philip baptised him. When they came up out of the water, the Spirit of the Lord took Philip away.

The official did not see him again, but continued on his way, full of joy.

Philip found himself in Azotus; he went on to Caesarea, and on the way he preached the Good News in every town.

# HOT-FOOT PHIL!

*This* Bible bit stars a guy called **Philip** (but *you* can call him Phil) who was to-ing and fro-ing all over the place telling people about **Jesus** and how Jesus was the Son of God.

One *particular* day, Philip had a surprise visit from none other than an **angel** from God who had a bit of work for Philip to do. The angel instructed our Phil to **hot-foot it** to a specific road (between Jerusalem and Gaza – you don't need to know *where* this is - it's not a geography lesson) and to wait for further instructions.

Meanwhile, one of the queen of Ethiopia's **top officials** was heading (in his rather posh carriage) down this very *same* road, on his way home from a trip to Jerusalem. Time for Philip's *next* intsruction but *this* time there wasn't an angel in sight.

Instead, this time it was the **Holy Spirit** who told our main man (Philip) what he had to do. 'Go over to that carriage and stay close to it.' As Philip ran alongside the carriage he overheard the Ethopian official reading from Bible book **Isaiah**.

Fortunately for puffed-out Philip, he didn't have to explain things while he jogged along bedside the carriage – the official kindly gave him a lift.

As it was, the official just happened to reading a Bible bit that was all about **Jesus.** The *good* news was that the Ethopian official believed everything that Philip said (*and* the stuff that he'd read in Isaiah) and decided, then and there, to become a follower of Jesus.

Not only *that* but he was dead set on getting **baptised** (dunked in water to show that Jesus has washed away all the bad in your life) **a.s.a.p.** (**a**s **s**oon **a**s **p**ossible). Stopping at a **handy desert pool**, Philip baptised his travelling companion and then . . . **disappeared**! Just like that!

The Bible tells us that Philip ended up in a place called Azotus. How did that happen? Only *God* knows. But one thing we *do* know is that the Ethopian official was overjoyed with his new life as a follower of Jesus.

# SAUL'S CONVERSION

## WHAT'S IT ALL ABOUT?

This Bible story is about how Saul, an enemy of the followers of Jesus, became one of their number

## WHO ARE THE MAIN CHARACTERS?

Saul, his travelling companions and of course, Jesus

## WHERE'S IT FOUND IN THE BIBLE?

Acts 9:1-19

## HERE'S THE BIBLE PASSAGE...

In the meantime Saul kept up his violent threats of murder against the followers of the Lord. He went to the High Priest and asked for letters of introduction to the synagogues in Damascus, so that if he should find there any followers of the Way of the Lord, he would be able to arrest them, both men and women, and bring them back to Jerusalem.

As Saul was coming near the city of Damascus, suddenly a light from the sky flashed round him. He fell to the ground and heard a voice saying to him, 'Saul, Saul! Why do you persecute me?'

'Who are you, Lord?' he asked.

'I am Jesus, whom you persecute,' the voice said.

'But get up and go into the city, where you will be told what you must do.'

The men who were travelling with Saul had stopped, not saying a word; they heard the voice but could not see anyone. Saul got up from the ground and opened his eyes, but could not see a thing. So they took him by the hand and led him into Damascus. For three days he was not able to see, and during that time he did not eat or drink anything.

There was a believer in Damascus named Ananias. He had a vision, in which the Lord said to him,

'Ananias!'

'Here I am, Lord,' he answered.

The Lord said to him, 'Get ready and go to Straight Street, and at the house of Judas ask for a man from Tarsus named Saul. He is praying, and in a vision he has seen a man named Ananias come in and place his hands on him so that he might see again.'

Ananias answered, 'Lord, many people have told me about this man and about all the terrible things he has done to your people in Jerusalem. And he has come to Damascus with authority from the chief priests to arrest all who worship you.'

The Lord said to him, 'Go, because I have chosen him to serve me, to make my name known to Gentiles and kings and to the people of Israel.

'And I myself will show him all that he must suffer for my sake.'

So Ananias went, entered the house where Saul was, and placed his hands on him. 'Brother Saul,' he said, 'the Lord has sent me – Jesus himself, who appeared to you on the road as you were coming here.

'He sent me so that you might see again and be filled with the Holy Spirit.'

At once something like fish scales fell from Saul's eyes, and he was able to see again. He stood up and was baptised; and after he had eaten, his strength came back.

# STRUCK BLIND!

**Saul** was the sort of man that any follower of **Jesus** would most definitely *not* want to meet on a dark night. He hated anything and everything to do with Jesus – and that included **Jesus' followers**.

Saul had made it his business to hunt down anybody who claimed to be a member of Jesus' church and now he was getting ready to track down any of them who might be holed up in nearby **Damascus**.

Armed with letters of introduction to the synagogues (the Jewish churches) Saul set out with his travelling companions.

But one thing Saul *hadn't* bargained on was meeting up with Jesus *himself* along the way.

Just before he *got* to Damascus, a light so bright that even the **world's brightest floodlights** wouldn't be a patch on it, flashed all around him.

What happened *next* shocked Saul even more.

Jesus actually spoke to him . . .

Jesus told Saul to continue on to Damascus where he would then be told what to do next.

Saul had been temporarily **blinded** so his travelling companions had to lead him all the way.

For three long days, Saul ate nothing and for that matter *saw* nothing. Meanwhile, in a vision, God instructed one of these followers of Jesus (also called **Christians**), a man named **Ananias**, to go and place his hands on Saul so that he would see again. No *way* was Ananias looking forward to meeting up with his **arch-enemy**, Saul, but nevertheless Ananias obeyed God.

Sure enough, when Ananias did as God told him Saul got his sight back again.

Did Saul immediately grab Ananias and have him thrown in jail for being a Christian?

Nope! Saul became a Christian *himself*!

Now *there's* a turn-up for the books.

# PETER IN LYDDA AND JOPPA

## WHAT'S IT ALL ABOUT?

This Bible story is about how Peter heals a paralysed man and then restores the life of a dead woman

## WHO ARE THE MAIN CHARACTERS?

Peter, Aeneas, Tabitha and some weeping and wailing mourners

## WHERE'S IT FOUND IN THE BIBLE?

Acts 9:32-43

## HERE'S THE BIBLE PASSAGE...

Peter travelled everywhere, and on one occasion he went to visit God's people who lived in Lydda. There he met a man named Aeneas, who was paralysed and had not been able to get out of bed for eight years. 'Aeneas,' Peter said to him, 'Jesus Christ makes you well. Get up and make your bed.' At once Aeneas got up. All the people living in Lydda and Sharon saw him, and they turned to the Lord.

In Joppa there was a woman named Tabitha, who was a believer. (Her name in Greek is Dorcas, meaning 'a deer'.)

She spent all her time doing good and helping the poor. At that time she became ill and died. Her body was washed and laid in a room upstairs.

Joppa was not very far from Lydda, and when the believers in Joppa heard that Peter was in Lydda, they sent two men to him with the message, 'Please hurry and come to us.'

So Peter got ready and went with them. When he arrived, he was taken to the room upstairs, where all the widows crowded round him, crying and showing him all the shirts and coats that Dorcas had made while she was alive.

Peter put them all out of the room, and knelt down and prayed; then he turned to the body and said, 'Tabitha, get up!'

She opened her eyes, and when she saw Peter, she sat up. Peter reached over and helped her get up.

Then he called all the believers, including the widows, and presented her alive to them. The news about this spread all over Joppa, and many people believed in the Lord.

Peter stayed on in Joppa for many days with a tanner of leather named Simon.

# DEAD LUCKY!

You've probably heard of **Peter** – he was one of Jesus' disciples.

Peter was following in Jesus' footsteps and went around telling people about God, healing the sick and bringing the dead back to life (just like **Jesus** had *told* him to do).

Nothing was too much trouble for Jesus' main man and Peter was *forever* **criss-crossing** from one place to the another doing Jesus' business.

*One* time, Peter ended up at a town called **Lydda** where he'd gone to meet up with the Christians (followers of Jesus) who lived there.

When Peter was introduced to a man (**Aeneas**) who'd been paralysed and bed-bound for **eight years** it wasn't *sympathy* that Peter gave him.

'Aeneas, Jesus Christ makes you well. Get up and make your bed.'

And guess what? Aeneas got up! (And presumably made his bed as well – let's just hope that this wasn't the *first* time it had been made in eight years, eh? Yuk!)

As a result of that miracle the Bible says that *all* the inhabitants of Lydda became Christians.

Next up, Peter moved on to a place called **Joppa** where *another* miracle was just waiting to happen. A generous and kind Christian lady (**Tabitha**) had fallen ill and died.

When news got out that Peter was in town he was hurriedly taken into the house where her body lay. First things first, Peter cleared all the weeping and wailing friends and relatives from the room.

With a bit of peace and quiet to concentrate, Peter knelt down, prayed to God and then had a quick word with Tabitha . . .

No arguing with *that* is there?

Lo and behold, Tabitha opened her eyes and sat up.

What a **fortunate** lady she was (but most certainly *not* lucky and now most definitely *not* dead). When news got out of this miracle even *more* people became followers of Jesus.

Two miracles – *loads* of Christians! That's what I *call* a good result.

# PETER AND CORNELIUS

## WHAT'S IT ALL ABOUT?

This Bible story is about how Peter is convinced that God loves the Gentiles as well as the Jews

## WHO ARE THE MAIN CHARACTERS?

Peter, Cornelius, a sheet-full of assorted creatures and hospitable Simon the tanner

## WHERE'S IT FOUND IN THE BIBLE?

Acts 10:1-28 and 44-48

## HERE'S THE BIBLE PASSAGE...

There was a man in Caesarea named Cornelius, who was a captain in the Roman regiment called 'The Italian Regiment'. He was a religious man; he and his whole family worshipped God. He also did much to help the Jewish poor people and was constantly praying to God. It was about three o'clock one afternoon when he had a vision, in which he clearly saw an angel of God come in and say to him, 'Cornelius!'

He stared at the angel in fear and said, 'What is it, sir?' The angel answered, 'God is pleased with your prayers and works of charity, and is ready to answer you. And now send some men to Joppa for a certain man whose full name is Simon Peter. He is a guest in the home of a tanner of leather named Simon, who lives by the sea.'

Then the angel went away, and Cornelius called two of his house servants and a soldier, a religious man who was one of his personal attendants. He told them what had happened and sent them off to Joppa. The next day, as they were on their way and coming near Joppa, Peter went up on the roof of the house about noon in order to pray.

He became hungry and wanted something to eat; while the food was being prepared, he had a vision. He saw heaven opened and something coming down that looked like a large sheet being lowered by its four corners to the earth. In it were all kinds of animals, reptiles, and wild birds. A voice said to him, 'Get up, Peter; kill and eat!'

But Peter said, 'Certainly not, Lord! I have never eaten anything ritually unclean or defiled.'

The voice spoke to him again, 'Do not consider anything unclean that God has declared clean.' This happened three times, and then the thing was taken back up into heaven. While Peter was wondering about the meaning of this vision, the men sent by Cornelius had learnt where Simon's house was, and they were now standing in front of the gate. They called out and asked, 'Is there a guest here by the name of Simon Peter?'

Peter was still trying to understand what the vision meant, when the Spirit said, 'Listen! Three men are here looking for you. So get ready and go down, and do not hesitate to go with them, for I have sent them.' So Peter went down and said to the men, 'I am the man you are looking for. Why have you come?'

'Captain Cornelius sent us,' they answered. 'He is a good man who worships God and is highly respected by all the Jewish people. An angel of God told him to invite you to his house, so that he could hear what you have to say.' Peter invited the men in and persuaded them to spend the night there.

The next day he got ready and went with them; and some of the believers from Joppa went along with him. The following day he arrived in Caesarea, where Cornelius was waiting for him, together with relatives and close friends that he had invited.

As Peter was about to go in, Cornelius met him, fell at his feet, and bowed down before him. But Peter made him rise. 'Stand up,' he said; 'I myself am only a man.' Peter kept on talking to Cornelius as he went into the house, where he found many people gathered. He said to them, 'You yourselves know very well that a Jew is not allowed by his religion to visit or associate with Gentiles. But God has shown me that I must not consider any person ritually unclean or defiled.'

While Peter was still speaking, the Holy Spirit came down on all those who were listening to his message. The Jewish believers were amazed that God had poured out his gift of the Holy Spirit on the Gentiles too. For they also heard them speaking in strange tongues and praising God's greatness.

Peter spoke up: 'These people have received the Holy Spirit, just as we also did. Can anyone stop them from being baptised with water?'

So he ordered them to be baptised in the name of Jesus Christ.

# FOOD FOR THOUGHT!

A couple of thousand years back, the **Romans** were *everywhere* (well, almost).

Although they'd conquered *heaps* of places they weren't *all* bad. *This* Bible bit features a Roman captain who went by the name of **Cornelius**. He (and his family) worshipped God which is probably why God chose to show up to him in **a vision** (which is a sort of dream).

Cornelius was busily praying away one afternoon when he saw, as clear as crystal, **an angel from God**. The angel called him by name and told him that God was well aware of his prayers and his generosity and *now* God wanted him to fetch a Christian called **Peter**.

Being a rather helpful angel, he gave Cornelius the address where Peter was staying – 'The home of Simon the tanner, By the sea, Joppa.'

Cornelius wasted no time in dispatching two of his most **trusted servants** to find Peter and bring him back. But Peter was about to have a vision of his very *own*. While he was up on the roof (they had flat ones in those days) in the middle of his midday prayer time, Peter started to feel a bit peckish.

Suddenly he had a vision where he saw heaven opened and a **large sheet** being lowered which was **jam-packed full** of all sorts of animals, birds and reptiles.

Then God spoke to Peter . . .

But God wasn't to be trifled with. God told Peter that from now on *nothing* was to be thought of as ritually unclean.

(The Jewish Law forbade Jews from eating certain animals and called them 'unclean'.) God was now saying that this was **a thing of the past**. From now on, nothing (or *nobody*) was excluded from God. God wasn't *just* for the Jewish people but for **everybody**.

Cornelius' servants took Peter back to Cornelius where both men shared their amazing visions.

Just to prove that God's love was open to both Jews and **Gentiles** (*non*-Jews) God's Holy Spirit filled everyone in Cornelius' house.

To put the final seal on the day, all the Gentiles were baptised.

# PETER IN PRISON

## WHAT'S IT ALL ABOUT?

This Bible story is about an angel's audacious rescue of Peter from inside a prison

## WHO ARE THE MAIN CHARACTERS?

Peter, an angel, some unfortunate prison guards and an excitable servant girl called Rhoda

## WHERE'S IT FOUND IN THE BIBLE?

Acts 12:1-19

## HERE'S THE BIBLE PASSAGE...

About this time King Herod began to persecute some members of the church. He had James, the brother of John, put to death by the sword. When he saw that this pleased the Jews, he went on to arrest Peter.

(This happened during the time of the Festival of Unleavened Bread.) After his arrest Peter was put in jail, where he was handed over to be guarded by four groups of four soldiers each. Herod planned to put him on trial in public after Passover. So Peter was kept in jail, but the people of the church were praying earnestly to God for him.

The night before Herod was going to bring him out to the people, Peter was sleeping between two guards. He was tied with two chains, and there were guards on duty at the prison gate. Suddenly an angel of the Lord stood there, and a light shone in the cell. The angel shook Peter by the shoulder, woke him up, and said, 'Hurry! Get up!' At once the chains fell off Peter's hands.

Then the angel said, 'Fasten your belt and put on your sandals.' Peter did so, and the angel said, 'Put your cloak round you and come with me.' Peter followed him out of the prison, not knowing, however, if what the angel was doing was real; he thought he was seeing a vision. They passed by the first guard post and then the second, and came at last to the iron gate leading into the city. The gate opened for them by itself, and they went out.

They walked down a street, and suddenly the angel left Peter. Then Peter realised what had happened to him, and said, 'Now I know that it is really true! The Lord sent his angel to rescue me from Herod's power and from everything the Jewish people expected to happen.'

Aware of his situation, he went to the home of Mary, the mother of John Mark, where many people had gathered and were praying. Peter knocked at the outside door, and a servant named Rhoda came to answer it. She recognised Peter's voice and was so happy that she ran back in without opening the door, and announced that Peter was standing outside. 'You are mad!' they told her. But she insisted that it was true. So they answered, 'It is his angel.'

Meanwhile Peter kept on knocking. At last they opened the door, and when they saw him, they were amazed.

He motioned with his hand for them to be quiet, and he explained to them how the Lord had brought him out of prison. 'Tell this to James and the rest of the believers,' he said; then he left and went somewhere else.

When morning came, there was a tremendous confusion among the guards – what had happened to Peter? Herod gave orders to search for him, but they could not find him.

So he had the guards questioned and ordered them to be put to death. After this, Herod left Judea and spent some time in Caesarea.

# THE GREAT ESCAPE!

Things were *really* hotting up for the **Christians** who lived shorly after Jesus' death. The more *good* they did the more enemies they seemed to *make*.

And *one* of those enemies was **King Herod**. He *hated* what these Christians did and said 'cos it put the spotlight on *his* wickedness – so he had one of their leaders (**James**) put to death by the sword. Which only goes to prove how wicked he really was, doesn't it?

When Herod realised that this met with the approval of the Jewish **religious leaders** (who despised the Christians as well) he had *another* of their leaders (**Peter**) arrested and locked up.

Just for the record, this wasn't Peter's *first* time in prison – the last time he was banged up, an angel of God came and rescued him. Just to be sure that history didn't repeat itself, **four groups of four soldiers** were put in charge of guarding Peter.

Peter was **chained up** to two of them and the other two stood guard at the **door**. Unfortunately for Herod, this wasn't gonna be his day because one thing he *hadn't* bargained on was Peter's friends from the church **praying for his release**.

Peter was woken from his slumbers by, yes, you guessed it, *another* **angel**. Okay it's predictable but I'll bet Peter's not complaining.

HURRY! GET UP! FASTEN YOUR BELT AND PUT ON YOUR SANDALS! PUT YOUR CLOAK ROUND YOU AND COME WITH ME.

The chains dropped off Peter's hands, just like that, and he was free.

The Bible says that Peter did exactly as he was told, but he wasn't sure if it was for *real* or if it was some sort of *vision*. The angel led Peter right past the guards without even a *murmur* from them.

Once he was outside, the angel disappeared and a rather bewildered Peter made his way to the house where all his friends were praying for him.

**Rat-a-tat-tat!** Peter knocked at the door. The servant-girl (**Rhoda**) who went to answer the door recognised Peter's voice and rushed back to tell everyone – forgetting to let Peter in!

Probably a bit over-excited wouldn't you say? When Peter finally *did* get let in everyone was **amazed**.

But when Herod found out he'd been **out-manoeuvred** he had the guards **executed**.

# ELYMAS THE MAGICIAN

## WHAT'S IT ALL ABOUT?

This Bible story is about how Saul and Barnabas confront Elymas the magician and how he comes a cropper

## WHO ARE THE MAIN CHARACTERS?

Saul, Barnabus, Elymas the magician and Sergius Paulus, the governor of Cyprus

## WHERE'S IT FOUND IN THE BIBLE?

Acts 13:4-12

## HERE'S THE BIBLE PASSAGE...

Having been sent by the Holy Spirit, Barnabas and Saul went to Seleucia and sailed from there to the island of Cyprus.

When they arrived at Salamis, they preached the word of God in the synagogues.

They had John Mark with them to help in the work.

They went all the way across the island to Paphos, where they met a certain magician named Bar-Jesus, a Jew who claimed to be a prophet. He was a friend of the governor of the island, Sergius Paulus, who was an intelligent man.

The governor called Barnabas and Saul before him because he wanted to hear the word of God. But they were opposed by the magician Elymas (that is his name in Greek), who tried to turn the governor away from the faith. Then Saul – also known as Paul – was filled with the Holy Spirit; he looked straight at the magician and said, 'You son of the Devil! You are the enemy of everything that is good.

'You are full of all kinds of evil tricks, and you always keep trying to turn the Lord's truths into lies! The Lord's hand will come down on you now; you will be blind and will not see the light of day for a time.'

At once Elymas felt a dark mist cover his eyes, and he walked about trying to find someone to lead him by the hand.

When the governor saw what had happened, he believed; for he was greatly amazed at the teaching about the Lord.

# DOUBLE ACT!

Here's a Bible bit about that famous Christian double-act, **Saul and Barnabas**. We catch up with this **no-nonsense duo** on the sunny Mediterranean island of **Cyprus** where they're about to have a bit of a head-to-head with the island's resident **magician**.

Saul and Barnabas had been doing a whistle-stop tour of the island, doing a spot of preaching in the Jewish synagogues along the way, and spreading the news that Jesus can change lives.

But for *some* Jews, the name of **Jesus** left a bad taste in their mouths and that *included* a guy called **Elymas**.

Elymas was a magician (or sorcerer) and was quite **pally-pally** with the island's governor, **Sergius Paulus**. The governor (so the Bible tells us) was a bit of a **smarty pants** (well actually it says that he was an intelligent man but it's the same thing, isn't it?).

When news reached him of Saul and Barnabas he wanted to hear, firsthand, what they had to say about God. Elymas didn't like this idea one little bit. If the governor bought into what this pair of Christians had to say, his days of influence on Cyprus might be numbered. Elymas tried to persuade Sergius Paulus not to listen to Saul and Barnabas.

Saul was having none of it!

YOU SON OF THE DEVIL! YOU ARE THE ENEMY OF EVERYTHING THAT IS GOOD. YOU ARE FULL OF ALL KINDS OF EVIL TRICKS AND YOU ALWAYS KEEP TRYING TO TURN THE LORD'S TRUTH INTO LIES! THE LORD'S HAND WILL COME DOWN ON YOU NOW AND YOU WILL BE BLIND AND WILL NOT SEE THE LIGHT OF DAY FOR A TIME.

The Bible says that Elymas felt a **dark mist** cover his eyes and he stumbled about trying to get someone to help him find his way around.

No surprises that the governor (being a smarty pants) recognised this was God's doing and became the very latest believer in God.

# PAUL AND BARNABAS WORSHIPPED

## WHAT'S IT ALL ABOUT?

This Bible story is about how Paul heals a lame man and is then worshipped, along with his companion Barnabas

## WHO ARE THE MAIN CHARACTERS?

Paul, Barnabas, a lame man, a crowd of locals and some rabble-rousing Jews

## WHERE'S IT FOUND IN THE BIBLE?

Acts 14:8-20

## HERE'S THE BIBLE PASSAGE...

In Lystra there was a man who had been lame from birth and had never been able to walk. He sat there and listened to Paul's words.

Paul saw that he believed and could be healed, so he looked straight at him and said in a loud voice, 'Stand up straight on your feet!' The man jumped up and started walking around. When the crowds saw what Paul had done, they started shouting in their own Lycaonian language, 'The gods have become like men and have come down to us!'

They gave Barnabas the name Zeus, and Paul the name Hermes, because he was the chief speaker. The priest of the god Zeus, whose temple stood just outside the town, brought bulls and flowers to the gate, for he and the crowds wanted to offer sacrifice to the apostles.

When Barnabas and Paul heard what they were about to do, they tore their clothes and ran into the middle of the crowd, shouting,

'Why are you doing this? We ourselves are only human beings like you!

'We are here to announce the Good News, to turn you away from these worthless things to the living God, who made heaven, earth, sea, and all that is in them. In the past he allowed all people to go their own way.

'But he has always given evidence of his existence by the good things he does: he gives you rain from heaven and crops at the right times; he gives you food and fills your hearts with happiness.' Even with these words the apostles could hardly keep the crowd from offering a sacrifice to them.

Some Jews came from Antioch in Pisidia and from Iconium; they won the crowd over to their side, stoned Paul and dragged him out of the town, thinking that he was dead.

But when the believers gathered round him, he got up and went back into the town. The next day he and Barnabas went to Derbe.

# MISTAKEN IDENTITY!

This Bible story is all about the time when **Paul** (previously called Saul) and **Barnabas** show up at a place called **Lystra** to do their stuff (preaching, healings, miracles etc).

While they talked to the locals about **Jesus** and how he'd made it possible to have a **clean slate** with God (to have all the bad stuff we've done erased, permanently) **a lame man** caught Paul's eye.

Not *literally*, of course. That would have been *very* painful. Paul could see that the lame man really, really, *really* believed that Jesus *could* heal him.

So, taking the bull by the horns, Paul commanded him to stand up on his feet. The lame man didn't need to be told *twice*. He was up on his feet **like a shot**.

And at *that*, the crowd suddenly went **wild**.

Paul and Barnabas were *mortified* – the crowd thought that Barnabas was the god **Zeus** and Paul was the god **Hermes**. This was terrible. This wasn't supposed to happen.

To add insult to injury, the priest of the nearby temple of Zeus brought bulls and flowers to them so that he could offer sacrifices to Paul and Barnabas. In despair, our dynamic duo **ripped their clothes** (as a sign that what was happening grieved them) and tried to shout over the **hullabaloo** that they **weren't** gods – they were ordinary people – and that the God who made the universe was the one they *should* be worshipping.

Their words fell on deaf ears. When a bunch of **trouble-making Jews** arrived on the scene they wasted no time in turning the crowd against Paul and Barnabas.

Paul ended up getting **stoned** and then left for **dead**. But fear not 'cos the Bible says that when some Christians gathered round Paul (presumably to pray for him) he got up.

Nothing daunted, the very next day, Paul and Barnabas were back on the road again. You just can't keep a good man (or two) down, can you?

# PAUL AND SILAS IN PRISON

## WHAT'S IT ALL ABOUT?

This Bible story is about the time Paul and Silas got thrown into jail and then God set them free, courtesy of a rather handy earthquake

## WHO ARE THE MAIN CHARACTERS?

Paul, Silas, a slave-girl, various officials and a terrified jailer

## WHERE'S IT FOUND IN THE BIBLE?

Acts 16:16-34

## HERE'S THE BIBLE PASSAGE...

One day as we were going to the place of prayer, we were met by a young servant woman who had an evil spirit that enabled her to predict the future.

She earned a lot of money for her owners by telling fortunes. She followed Paul and us, shouting, 'These men are servants of the Most High God! They announce to you how you can be saved!'

She did this for many days, until Paul became so upset that he turned round and said to the spirit, 'In the name of Jesus Christ I order you to come out of her!' The spirit went out of her that very moment.

When her owners realised that their chance of making money was gone, they seized Paul and Silas and dragged them to the authorities in the public square. They brought them before the Roman officials and said, 'These men are Jews, and they are causing trouble in our city. They are teaching customs that are against our law; we are Roman citizens, and we cannot accept these customs or practise them.' And the crowd joined in the attack against Paul and Silas.

Then the officials tore the clothes off Paul and Silas and ordered them to be whipped. After a severe beating, they were thrown into jail, and the jailer was ordered to lock them up tight.

Upon receiving this order, the jailer threw them into the inner cell and fastened their feet between heavy blocks of wood.

About midnight Paul and Silas were praying and singing hymns to God, and the other prisoners were listening to them. Suddenly there was a violent earthquake, which shook the prison to its foundations. At once all the doors opened, and the chains fell off all the prisoners. The jailer woke up, and when he saw the prison doors open, he thought that the prisoners had escaped; so he pulled out his sword and was about to kill himself. But Paul shouted at the top of his voice, 'Don't harm yourself! We are all here!'

The jailer called for a light, rushed in, and fell trembling at the feet of Paul and Silas. Then he led them out and asked, 'Sirs, what must I do to be saved?' They answered, 'Believe in the Lord Jesus, and you will be saved – you and your family.' Then they preached the word of the Lord to him and to all the others in his house. At that very hour of the night the jailer took them and washed their wounds; and he and all his family were baptised at once. Then he took Paul and Silas up into his house and gave them some food to eat. He and his family were filled with joy, because they now believed in God.

# QUAKE WITH FEAR!

Before **Paul** had become a Christian (that's someone who believes in Jesus) he'd gone by the name of **Saul**. (Hardly seems worth changing it for just *one letter* but that's not our concern.) As *Saul* he was a nasty piece of work and someone you wouldn't want to mess with (that's if you were a Christian). As *Paul* he *still* wasn't someone you'd wanna mess with (but only if you were an enemy of God).

Paul was in a place called **Philippi** where he (and a whole bunch of Christians – including the writer of this Bible bit) were going round telling people that Jesus was the Son of God and what that meant.

Day after day, they were followed round by a **slave-girl** who was controlled by an evil spirit that enabled her to predict the future. In fact, she was *so* good at it that she made her owners a **small fortune** (by *telling* fortunes). 'These men are servants of the Most High God! They are telling you how to be saved', she kept on saying wherever Paul and co. went. Okay, so it might have been *true* but the *way* she was saying it was putting everybody off what Paul had to say. Enough was enough!

It was time for Paul to take a bit of decisive action. 'In the name of Jesus Christ I order you to come out of her!' And with that, the evil spirit left the girl and in an instant her owners had lost a good source of income.

They were so *miffed* that they caused a near **riot** and as a result **Paul** and **Silas** (one of his companions) got thrown into jail (but not before they were given a severe flogging – what rotters).

Were Paul and Silas downcast? Not in the least. In fact, the Bible says that at midnight they were wide awake and **singing hymns to God**.

Fortunately for Paul and Silas, their stay in prison was cut short by a sudden **earthquake** (no doubt provided by God). As a result, all the doors flung open, all their chains fell off . . . and they were free to go. When the **jailer** realised that he was going to be put out of business, he whipped out his **sword** to kill himself. The Roman authorities would do it to him anyway for letting his prisoners escape so he might as well save them the trouble.

Paul stopped him just in the nick of time and pointed out that all the prisoners were **present and correct**.

The jailer was one step ahead of the game and realised that **God** was behind this whole earthquake thing. There and then he (*and* his whole family) handed over their lives to God and became Christians themselves.

# RIOT IN EPHESUS

## WHAT'S IT ALL ABOUT?

This Bible story is about how Paul nearly got lynched by a bunch of Artemis worshippers

## WHO ARE THE MAIN CHARACTERS?

Paul, some travelling companions, Demetrius the silversmith and a cool-headed town clerk

## WHERE'S IT FOUND IN THE BIBLE?

Acts 19:21-41

## HERE'S THE BIBLE PASSAGE...

After these things had happened, Paul made up his mind to travel through Macedonia and Achaia and go on to Jerusalem. 'After I go there,' he said, 'I must also see Rome.' So he sent Timothy and Erastus, two of his helpers, to Macedonia, while he spent more time in the province of Asia.

It was at this time that there was serious trouble in Ephesus because of the Way of the Lord. A certain silversmith named Demetrius made silver models of the temple of the goddess Artemis, and his business brought a great deal of profit to the workers. So he called them all together with others whose work was like theirs and said to them, 'Men, you know that our prosperity comes from this work. Now, you can see and hear for yourselves what this fellow Paul is doing. He says that gods made by human hands are not gods at all, and he has succeeded in convincing many people, both here in Ephesus and in nearly the whole province of Asia.

'There is the danger, then, that this business of ours will get a bad name. Not only that, but there is also the danger that the temple of the great goddess Artemis will come to mean nothing and that her greatness will be destroyed — the goddess worshipped by everyone in Asia and in all the world!'

As the crowd heard these words, they became furious and started shouting, 'Great is Artemis of Ephesus!' The uproar spread throughout the whole city. The mob seized Gaius and Aristarchus, two Macedonians who were travelling with Paul, and rushed with them to the theatre. Paul himself wanted to go before the crowd, but the believers would not let him. Some of the provincial authorities, who were his friends, also sent him a message begging him not to show himself in the theatre.

Meanwhile the whole meeting was in an uproar: some people were shouting one thing, others were shouting something else, because most of them did not even know why they had come together. Some of the people concluded that Alexander was responsible, since the Jews made him go up to the front.

Then Alexander motioned with his hand for the people to be silent, and he tried to make a speech of defence. But when they recognised that he was a Jew, they all shouted together the same thing for two hours: 'Great is Artemis of Ephesus!'

At last the town clerk was able to calm the crowd. 'Fellow-Ephesians!' he said. 'Everyone knows that the city of Ephesus is the keeper of the temple of the great Artemis and of the sacred stone that fell down from heaven. Nobody can deny these things. So then, you must calm down and not do anything reckless.

'You have brought these men here even though they have not robbed temples or said evil things about our goddess.

'If Demetrius and his workers have an accusation against anyone, we have the authorities and the regular days for court; charges can be made there.

'But if there is something more that you want, it will have to be settled in a legal meeting of citizens. For after what has happened today, there is the danger that we will be accused of a riot. There is no excuse for all this uproar, and we would not be able to give a good reason for it.'

After saying this, he dismissed the meeting.

# ART' ATTACK!

One of the most *famous* Christians (from long ago) was a guy called **Paul** who made it his business to travel back and forth around the sunny **Mediterranean** region telling all and sundry about Jesus and getting loads and loads of churches up and running at the same time.

One of these churches happened to be in a place called **Ephesus**, which is where we catch up with Paul now. But not *everybody* wanted to hear what Paul had to say.

*Lots* of the **Ephesians** (people who live in Ephesus) worshipped the goddess **Artemis** and the city even boasted a whopping big temple devoted to her.

Not wanting to miss out on a good business opportunity, **Demetrius** (a silversmith) made a jolly good living (for himself *and* his workers) making silver models of the temple.

The *last* thing they needed was this guy Paul turning the city away from Artemis to follow this God **Jesus**.

Demetrius stirred things up something rotten until nearly everyone in the city wanted to lynch Paul. The angry mob seized a couple of Christians and stormed the city's theatre. But it was Paul they *really* were after.

The chant went on for **two hours** – there was simply no shutting them up. Paul wanted to have it out with them face to face but it was too dangerous and he was stopped from going anywhere near the theatre.

Finally, it was left to the **town clerk** to bring some calm to the proceedings. He pointed out that if Demetrius had a gripe against Paul then he should take him to court – not start a riot.

And with that, he sent the crowd to their homes . . . and Paul lived to fight another day.

# EUTYCHUS

## WHAT'S IT ALL ABOUT?

This Bible story is about a young man who fell out of a window but lived to tell the tale

## WHO ARE THE MAIN CHARACTERS?

Paul, Eutychus and a bunch of believers

## WHERE'S IT FOUND IN THE BIBLE?

Acts 20:7-12

## HERE'S THE BIBLE PASSAGE...

On Saturday evening we gathered together for the fellowship meal. Paul spoke to the people and kept on speaking until midnight, since he was going to leave the next day. Many lamps were burning in the upstairs room where we were meeting.

A young man named Eutychus was sitting in the window, and as Paul kept on talking, Eutychus got sleepier and sleepier, until he finally went sound asleep and fell from the third storey to the ground.

When they picked him up, he was dead. But Paul went down and threw himself on him and hugged him. 'Don't worry,' he said, 'he is still alive!'

Then he went back upstairs, broke bread, and ate.

After talking with them for a long time, even until sunrise, Paul left. They took the young man home alive and were greatly comforted.

# THE FALL GUY!

*This* Bible story is all about the time that **Paul** (a Christian who spent most of his time travelling round doing stuff for Jesus) met up with a bunch of fellow Christians (in **Troas**) to have a nice **Saturday night dinner party**.

Paul was only in Troas for a week (as the Bible kindly informs us) and this was gonna be his last night in town. Not having the benefit of electricity, the upstairs room where they were all hanging out was lit by **oil lamps**.

I'll bet that it didn't take long for the room to become all **warm and cosy** with all those lamps blazing away. Which is probably *one* of the reasons for what happened next.

While Paul **talked and talked** . . . **and talked and talked**, a young man (**Eutychus**) started to get bleary eyed.

> YAWN! DON'T TAKE IT PERSONALLY PAUL! YOU'RE NOT BORING ME – HONEST!

To be fair, you can hardly blame the poor chap. It was midnight and it had no doubt been a long day. Unfortunately for Eutychus, he was perched on a **window ledge** so when sleep *finally* caught up with him and he dropped off to sleep, he *also* dropped off the window ledge (which was **two floors up**).

Everyone raced downstairs but Eutychus was **dead**. Paul wasn't put off by a trifling thing like *that*.

Paul threw himself on the young man and hugged him and with that, Eutychus **came back to life** again. Now that's what I *call* an unconventional miracle of God.

Did they pack Eutychus back off to his home to get some much-needed shut-eye? Nope! They all went back upstairs again and carried on until dawn.

At sunrise, Paul headed off on his travels, only *then* did Eutychus head for home.

What a night *that* had been.

# PAUL HEADS FOR JERUSALEM

## WHAT'S IT ALL ABOUT?

This Bible story is about how Paul is warned (twice) not to travel to Jerusalem but goes nevertheless

## WHO ARE THE MAIN CHARACTERS?

Paul, Agabus and a mixed assortment of believers

## WHERE'S IT FOUND IN THE BIBLE?

Acts 21:1-15

## HERE'S THE BIBLE PASSAGE...

We said goodbye to them and left. After sailing straight across, we came to Cos; the next day we reached Rhodes, and from there we went on to Patara. There we found a ship that was going to Phoenicia, so we went aboard and sailed away.

We came to where we could see Cyprus, and then sailed south of it on to Syria. We went ashore at Tyre, where the ship was going to unload its cargo. There we found some believers and stayed with them a week.

By the power of the Spirit they told Paul not to go to Jerusalem. But when our time with them was over, we left and went on our way. All of them, together with their wives and children, went with us out of the city to the beach, where we all knelt and prayed. Then we said goodbye to one another, and we went on board the ship while they went back home.

We continued our voyage, sailing from Tyre to Ptolemais, where we greeted the believers and stayed with them for a day. On the following day we left and arrived in Caesarea. There we stayed at the house of Philip the evangelist, one of the seven men who had been chosen as helpers in Jerusalem. He had four unmarried daughters who proclaimed God's message.

We had been there for several days when a prophet named Agabus arrived from Judea.

He came to us, took Paul's belt, tied up his own feet and hands with it, and said, 'This is what the Holy Spirit says: The owner of this belt will be tied up in this way by the Jews in Jerusalem, and they will hand him over to the Gentiles.'

When we heard this, we and the others there begged Paul not to go to Jerusalem. But he answered, 'What are you doing, crying like this and breaking my heart? I am ready not only to be tied up in Jerusalem but even to die there for the sake of the Lord Jesus.' We could not convince him, so we gave up and said, 'May the Lord's will be done.'

After spending some time there, we got our things ready and left for Jerusalem.

# DON'T GO!

Paul (the famous Christian) was not a man to be easily side-tracked. *This* Bible bit is all about when he was headed for **Jerusalem** (the capital city of Israel) to meet up with some of the *other* followers of Jesus who lived there.

Paul was making the journey by boat ('cos planes hadn't been invented yet). The boat stopped off at a place called **Tyre** to unload its cargo, so Paul took time out with some of the Christians who live there.

When the time finally came to leave Tyre, Paul's new-found friends urged him not to go to Jerusalem. They sensed that God was telling Paul that this wasn't a good idea.

But Paul was *not* gonna be put off. He bade them farewell and continued on his merry way. After a bit more travelling Paul arrived in **Caesarea** where he was provided with bed and board by a fella called **Philip the evangelist** (also a follower of Jesus).

Then, seven days later, an unexpected visitor from out of town arrived. It was **Agabus** (a prophet of God from Judea).

Agabus had a message for Paul which went something like this . . .

That was the *second* time Paul had been warned about the dangers that awaited him in Jerusalem but even though everyone *begged* him not to go, Paul refused to be put off.

'I am ready not only to be *tied up* in Jerusalem but even to **die** there for the sake of the **Lord Jesus**', Paul told them.

Once they realised that nothing but *nothing* was gonna stop Paul they sent him on his way with their blessing.

# PAUL ARRESTED

**WHAT'S IT ALL ABOUT?**

This Bible story is about when Paul arrived in Jerusalem only to end up almost getting killed by a mob of angry Jews

**WHO ARE THE MAIN CHARACTERS?**

Paul, some Jews from a province of Asia and a timely Roman commander

**WHERE'S IT FOUND IN THE BIBLE?**

Acts 21:27-36 and 22:30

## HERE'S THE BIBLE PASSAGE...

But just when the seven days were about to come to an end, some Jews from the province of Asia saw Paul in the Temple. They stirred up the whole crowd and seized Paul. 'Men of Israel!' they shouted. 'Help! This is the man who goes everywhere teaching everyone against the people of Israel, the Law of Moses, and this Temple.

'And now he has even brought some Gentiles into the Temple and defiled this holy place!' (They said this because they had seen Trophimus from Ephesus with Paul in the city, and they thought that Paul had taken him into the Temple.)

Confusion spread through the whole city, and the people all ran together, seized Paul, and dragged him out of the Temple. At once the Temple doors were closed. The mob was trying to kill Paul, when a report was sent up to the commander of the Roman troops that all Jerusalem was rioting. At once the commander took some officers and soldiers and rushed down to the crowd. When the people saw him with the soldiers, they stopped beating Paul.

The commander went over to Paul, arrested him, and ordered him to be bound with two chains.

Then he asked, 'Who is this man, and what has he done?'

Some in the crowd shouted one thing, others something else. There was such confusion that the commander could not find out exactly what had happened, so he ordered his men to take Paul up into the fort.

They got as far as the steps with him, and then the soldiers had to carry him because the mob was so wild. They were all coming after him and screaming, 'Kill him!' The commander wanted to find out for certain what the Jews were accusing Paul of; so the next day he had Paul's chains taken off and ordered the chief priests and the whole Council to meet.

Then he took Paul and made him stand before them.

# MAUL PAUL!

If you know *anything* about **Jesus** and the **Bible** then you'll probably be aware that the mere *mention* of Jesus can cause *some* people to get a bit **hot under the collar**. That *included* many **Jews** who were dead against anything (or *anyone*) to do with Jesus. And that included **Paul**.

Paul was brought up a Jew but had come to realise that the Jewish religion was only the **big build-up** to Jesus. Paul was now a Christian and a radical follower of Jesus.

As far as *most* Jews were concerned, Paul was **a traitor** so when he showed up in Jerusalem (the Jews' main city) word soon got out that this turncoat was in town.

For *his* part Paul made a big thing about trying *not* to do anything that would cause offence to the Jews and their religion.

But for *their* part the Jews were looking for anything that even *hinted* of breaking their laws. Finally they had something. Rumour had it that Paul had taken a **Gentile** (someone who *wasn't* a Jew) into the Jews' **Temple** in Jerusalem. This was one **big no-no**!

What they'd *actually* seen was Paul walking round the city with a guy called **Trophimus** (a Gentile) but those angry Jews weren't really interested in the truth. They wanted Paul's **guts for garters** and by hook or by crook they were gonna get 'em!

Paul was dragged out of the Temple (where he *was* at *that* particular moment) and they laid into him. The **Roman commander** of the city soon got wind that a near *riot* was on his hands and had Paul plucked from the seething mob just in the nick of time.

For some unapparent reason, Paul was bound in chains and arrested *before* he was whisked away to the nearby Roman fort for his safety.

Even *that* didn't stop the Jews chasing after Paul and screaming 'Kill him!' Not very nice, is it?

Next day, **beaten** and **bruised**, Paul finally had his chains removed because the time had come for Paul to defend himself before the Jewish Council and chief priests.

# PAUL ON TRIAL

## WHAT'S IT ALL ABOUT?

This Bible story is about how Paul sought to defend himself against the wrath of the Jews

## WHO ARE THE MAIN CHARACTERS?

Paul, the High Priest, and some feuding Pharisees and Sadducees

## WHERE'S IT FOUND IN THE BIBLE?

Acts 23:1-11

## HERE'S THE BIBLE PASSAGE...

Paul looked straight at the Council and said, 'My fellow-Israelites! My conscience is perfectly clear about the way in which I have lived before God to this very day.' The High Priest Ananias ordered those who were standing close to Paul to strike him on the mouth.

Paul said to him, 'God will certainly strike you – you whitewashed wall! You sit there to judge me according to the Law, yet you break the Law by ordering them to strike me!'

The men close to Paul said to him, 'You are insulting God's High Priest!' Paul answered, 'My fellow-Israelites, I did not know that he was the High Priest.

'The scripture says, "You must not speak evil of the ruler of your people."'

When Paul saw that some of the group were Sadducees and the others were Pharisees, he called out in the Council, 'Fellow-Israelites! I am a Pharisee, the son of Pharisees. I am on trial here because of the hope I have that the dead will rise to life!'

As soon as he said this, the Pharisees and Sadducees started to quarrel, and the group was divided. (For the Sadducees say that people will not rise from death and that there are no angels or spirits; but the Pharisees believe in all three.)

The shouting became louder, and some of the teachers of the Law who belonged to the party of the Pharisees stood up and protested strongly:

'We cannot find anything wrong with this man! Perhaps a spirit or an angel really did speak to him!'

The argument became so violent that the commander was afraid that Paul would be torn to pieces.

So he ordered his soldiers to go down into the group, get Paul away from them, and take him into the fort.

That night the Lord stood by Paul and said, 'Don't be afraid! You have given your witness for me here in Jerusalem, and you must also do the same in Rome.'

# TRIAL...RUN!

At long last, the **Jewish authorities** had got their man. They'd been trying to get their hands on a chap called **Paul** (a Christian leader) for *ages* so that they could put him on trial for turning people against the Jewish religion (which, to be fair to Paul, he hadn't) and finally, the moment they'd all been waiting for had arrived.

With a **guard of Roman soldiers** on hand just in case these Jews turned angry (as they'd done on *many* an occasion) Paul started to lay out his defence before the assembled **Council**.

Before he'd even had the chance to say more than a short sentence, the High Priest (**Ananias**) ordered those standing near to Paul to **strike him on the mouth**. Paul was none too pleased.

GOD WILL CERTAINLY STRIKE YOU, YOU WHITEWASHED WALL! YOU SIT THERE TO JUDGE ME ACCORDING TO THE LAW YET YOU BREAK IT BY ORDERING THEM TO STRIKE ME!

When Paul realised that it was the *High Priest* he was talking to, he apologised for stepping out of line.

And *then* Paul pulled his **master stroke**. He told the Council that he came from a family of **Pharisees** (one of the main religious groups) and that the only reason he was on trial was because he believed that the dead will one day rise to life (which is what the Pharisees *also* believed).

Where they *differed* is that Paul believed that Jesus had *also* risen from the dead but he didn't need to say any more because an argument was about to erupt in which *his* input *wasn't* required.

The **Sadducees** (*another* group of Jews) didn't believe in *anything* like that at all, which set them off in a war of words with the Pharisees.

As the argument reached **fever pitch** the Pharisees started to side with Paul. This was like a red rag to a bull for the Sadducees – they were **furious**.

The Roman commander, sensing that any moment now Paul was going to get torn to pieces, ordered his men to **get Paul outta there** right now!

Phew! *That* was close.

Back in the safety of the Roman fort, Paul had a personal visit from God.

'Don't be afraid! You have given your witness for me here in Jerusalem and now you must also do the same in Rome.' Looks to me like Paul's gonna be on the move *again* don't you think?

# A PLOT AGAINST PAUL

## WHAT'S IT ALL ABOUT?

This Bible story is about a plot by the Jews to kill Paul and how his sharp-thinking nephew saves the day

## WHO ARE THE MAIN CHARACTERS?

Paul, his nephew, forty plus plotting Jews and 470 Roman troops

## WHERE'S IT FOUND IN THE BIBLE?

Acts 23:12-24

## HERE'S THE BIBLE PASSAGE...

The next morning some Jews met together and made a plan. They took a vow that they would not eat or drink anything until they had killed Paul.

There were more than forty who planned this together.

Then they went to the chief priests and elders and said, 'We have taken a solemn vow together not to eat a thing until we have killed Paul.

'Now then, you and the Council send word to the Roman commander to bring Paul down to you, pretending that you want to get more accurate information about him. But we will be ready to kill him before he ever gets here.'

But the son of Paul's sister heard about the plot; so he went to the fort and told Paul.

Then Paul called one of the officers and said to him, 'Take this young man to the commander; he has something to tell him.'

The officer took him, led him to the commander, and said, 'The prisoner Paul called me and asked me to bring this young man to you, because he has something to say to you.'

The commander took him by the hand, led him off by himself, and asked him, 'What have you got to tell me?'

He said, 'The Jewish authorities have agreed to ask you tomorrow to take Paul down to the Council, pretending that the Council wants to get more accurate information about him. But don't listen to them, because there are more than forty men who will be hiding and waiting for him. They have taken a vow not to eat or drink until they have killed him. They are now ready to do it and are waiting for your decision.'

The commander said, 'Don't tell anyone that you have reported this to me.' And he sent the young man away.

Then the commander called two of his officers and said, 'Get two hundred soldiers ready to go to Caesarea, together with seventy horsemen and two hundred spearmen, and be ready to leave by nine o'clock tonight. Provide some horses for Paul to ride and get him safely through to the governor Felix.'

# LOST THE PLOT!

Things are *really* starting to hot up in *this* bit of the Bible and it all revolves around an obstinate and uncompromising follower of Jesus called **Paul**. The Christians *love* him, the Jews *hate* him and the Romans haven't a clue what to *do* with him.

Right now, Paul is up to his neck in it. While *he's* safely tucked away in a **Roman fort** (in Jerusalem) a gang of **angry Jews** (over forty of them, if you *must* know) have gone and made a vow not to eat *anything* until they've killed Paul.

Their **sneaky plan** was to persuade the Roman commander to release Paul under the pretence that they wanted to ask him a few questions.

Sounds pretty harmless except for the fact that they were *really* planning to ambush Paul (along the way) and **kill him**. But don't panic – all is not lost!

The Bible says that **Paul's sister** got wind of the plot and sent her **son** (Paul's **nephew** – hope you're not *too* confused) to warn Paul immediately.

When the Roman commander heard what Paul's nephew had to say, he took immediate action. Paul was gonna be sent to the governor of Caesarea (Felix) for his own safety.

At nine o'clock that night, along with **200** soldiers, **200** spearmen and **70** horsemen (nothing like travelling light is there?) Paul was escorted (under cover of darkness) away from Jerusalem. Who *knows* whether or not those **scheming plotters** gave up on their vow. If they didn't then they were sure gonna be hungry!

# PAUL APPEALS TO THE EMPEROR

## WHAT'S IT ALL ABOUT?

This Bible story is about how Paul resorts to standing trial before the Roman Emperor to thwart the Jews' plan to kill him

## WHO ARE THE MAIN CHARACTERS?

Paul, Festus the governor of Caesarea and the usual bunch of seething Jews

## WHERE'S IT FOUND IN THE BIBLE?

Acts 25:1-12

## HERE'S THE BIBLE PASSAGE...

Three days after Festus arrived in the province, he went from Caesarea to Jerusalem, where the chief priests and the Jewish leaders brought their charges against Paul. They begged Festus to do them the favour of bringing Paul to Jerusalem, for they had made a plot to kill him on the way.

Festus answered, 'Paul is being kept a prisoner in Caesarea, and I myself will be going back there soon. Let your leaders go to Caesarea with me and accuse the man if he has done anything wrong.'

Festus spent another eight or ten days with them and then went to Caesarea. On the next day he sat down in the court of judgement and ordered Paul to be brought in. When Paul arrived, the Jews who had come from Jerusalem stood round him and started making many serious charges against him, which they were not able to prove.

But Paul defended himself: 'I have done nothing wrong against the Law of the Jews or against the Temple or against the Roman Emperor.'

But Festus wanted to gain favour with the Jews, so he asked Paul, 'Would you be willing to go to Jerusalem and be tried on these charges before me there?'

Paul said, 'I am standing before the Emperor's own court of judgement, where I should be tried. I have done no wrong to the Jews, as you yourself well know. If I have broken the law and done something for which I deserve the death penalty, I do not ask to escape it. But if there is no truth in the charges they bring against me, no one can hand me over to them. I appeal to the Emperor.'

Then Festus, after conferring with his advisers, answered, 'You have appealed to the Emperor, so to the Emperor you will go.'

# APPEALING PAUL!

There's one thing about **God** that you should know and it's this. When God *says* something's gonna happen – it'll *happen*! God had told the star of *this* Bible story (a Christian called **Paul**) that one day he'd end up in **Rome** so's he could tell the people there all the brill stuff about Jesus that they needed to know. *This* Bible bit is about when Paul **books his ticket** (not literally of course!).

Paul had been under lock and key in the city of **Caesarea** for two long years (mainly to protect him from his enemies, the Jews, who wanted him dead).

A new governor (**Festus**) had just arrived and the Jews wasted *no* time in trying to convince Festus to send Paul back to **Jerusalem** for a proper trial according to their *Jewish* laws (so they could kill him along the way). First off, Festus had Paul brought before him to hear what *he* had to say . . .

> I HAVE DONE NOTHING WRONG AGAINST THE LAW OF THE JEWS OR AGAINST THE TEMPLE OR AGAINST THE ROMAN EMPEROR!

. . . which was perfectly true.

But, being *new* in the job, Festus wanted to get in with the Jews so he went along with their **conniving little scheme**.

Paul, for *his* part, was having *none* of it. He figured that 'cos he was in a **Roman court** he should be tried by the **Romans**.

In fact, why not go to the **very top**? Paul decided that there was only one way out of this – he demanded (as was the right of *every* Roman citizen – which Paul *was*) to stand trial before the **Emperor**. 'I appeal to the Emperor,' said Paul.

After a conflab with his advisers, Festus agreed to Paul's request. Look out Rome – here comes Paul!

# PAUL SETS SAIL FOR ROME

## WHAT'S IT ALL ABOUT?

This Bible story is about the first leg of Paul's sea voyage to Rome and the disastrous conditions he encountered

## WHO ARE THE MAIN CHARACTERS?

Paul, Julius a Roman officer, a ship-load of crew, soldiers and prisoners

## WHERE'S IT FOUND IN THE BIBLE?

Acts 27:1-26

## HERE'S THE BIBLE PASSAGE...

When it was decided that we should sail to Italy, they handed Paul and some other prisoners over to Julius, an officer in the Roman regiment called 'The Emperor's Regiment'. We went aboard a ship from Adramyttium, which was ready to leave for the seaports of the province of Asia, and we sailed away.

Aristarchus, a Macedonian from Thessalonica, was with us. The next day we arrived at Sidon. Julius was kind to Paul and allowed him to go and see his friends, to be given what he needed. We went on from there, and because the winds were blowing against us, we sailed on the sheltered side of the island of Cyprus. We crossed over the sea off Cilicia and Pamphylia and came to Myra in Lycia. There the officer found a ship from Alexandria that was going to sail for Italy, so he put us aboard.

We sailed slowly for several days and with great difficulty finally arrived off the town of Cnidus. The wind would not let us go any further in that direction, so we sailed down the sheltered side of the island of Crete, passing by Cape Salmone. We kept close to the coast and with great difficulty came to a place called Safe Harbours, not far from the town of Lasea.

We spent a long time there, until it became dangerous to continue the voyage, for by now the Day of Atonement was already past.

So Paul gave them this advice: 'Men, I see that our voyage from here on will be dangerous; there will be great damage to the cargo and to the ship, and loss of life as well.' But the army officer was convinced by what the captain and the owner of the ship said, and not by what Paul said. The harbour was not a good one to spend the winter in; so most people were in favour of putting out to sea and trying to reach Phoenix, if possible, in order to spend the winter there.

Phoenix is a harbour in Crete that faces south-west and north-west.

A soft wind from the south began to blow, and the men thought that they could carry out their plan, so they pulled up the anchor and sailed as close as possible along the coast of Crete.

But soon a very strong wind – the one called 'North-easter' – blew down from the island. It hit the ship, and since it was impossible to keep the ship headed into the wind, we gave up trying and let it be carried along by the wind. We got some shelter when we passed to the south of the little island of Cauda.

There, with some difficulty, we managed to make the ship's boat secure. They pulled it aboard and then fastened some ropes tight round the ship. They were afraid that they might run into the sandbanks off the coast of Libya, so they lowered the sail and let the ship be carried by the wind.

The violent storm continued, so on the next day they began to throw some of the ship's cargo overboard, and on the following day they threw part of the ship's equipment overboard. For many days we could not see the sun or the stars, and the wind kept on blowing very hard. We finally gave up all hope of being saved. After those on board had gone a long time without food, Paul stood before them and said, 'Men, you should have listened to me and not have sailed from Crete; then we would have avoided all this damage and loss.

'But now I beg you, take heart! Not one of you will lose your life; only the ship will be lost. For last night an angel of the God to whom I belong and whom I worship came to me and said, "Don't be afraid, Paul! You must stand before the Emperor. And God in his goodness to you has spared the lives of all those who are sailing with you." So take heart, men!

'For I trust in God that it will be just as I was told. But we will be driven ashore on some island.'

# THE RAGING STORM!

*This* Bible story is part one of a **sea voyage** that **Paul** (a Christian) was making to **Rome** where he was gonna stand trial before the **Roman Emperor**.

But first things first. From Israel to Rome was a whopper of a journey across the **Mediterranean Sea** and (as you're about to find out) it most definitely *wasn't* **plain sailing**.

Paul (along with loads of *other* prisoners) was under the watchful eye of a Roman commander called **Julius**. All seemed to be going well until they changed ships at a place called Lycia.

From then on in the voyage was slow going. Whichever way they turned the wind seemed to be against them. There was nothing for it but to edge slowly round the coast of Crete and hope for somewhere to anchor.

The ship eventually put in at a place called '**Safe Harbours**' and waited. But the storm just got worse. Paul had this warning for his shipmates . . .

> OUR VOYAGE FROM HERE WILL BE DANGEROUS. THERE WILL BE GREAT DAMAGE TO THE CARGO, TO THE SHIP AND LOSS OF LIFE AS WELL!

Nothing doing, Paul! The ship's captain was dead set on continuing with the voyage and that's what happened.

It was a big mistake though. Paul had been right. As the **doomed ship** headed out to sea, a wild wind blew up, so strong that the ship was tossed about all over the place. It was useless keeping the *sail* up, so down it came.

All aboard were now at the mercy of the raging sea. In desperation, the crew threw overboard anything they could think of to lighten the ship's load – cargo, equipment, it all had to go. The storm was now so bad that they couldn't see the sun or the stars – it was **blackness all around**.

Just when everyone thought that all was lost, Paul stood up and told them that he'd had a visit from an angel to say that **God** would protect them all from death and that they'd be **shipwrecked** on an island. Only the *ship* would be lost.

# THE SHIPWRECK

## WHAT'S IT ALL ABOUT?

This Bible story is about how Paul and his shipmates are washed ashore on the isalnd of Malta

## WHO ARE THE MAIN CHARACTERS?

Paul, his fellow-prisoners, the ship's crew and a load of Roman soldiers

## WHERE'S IT FOUND IN THE BIBLE?

Acts 27:27-44

## HERE'S THE BIBLE PASSAGE...

It was the fourteenth night, and we were being driven about in the Mediterranean by the storm. About midnight the sailors suspected that we were getting close to land. So they dropped a line with a weight tied to it and found that the water was 40 metres deep; a little later they did the same and found that it was 30 metres deep.

They were afraid that the ship would go on the rocks, so they lowered four anchors from the back of the ship and prayed for daylight. Then the sailors tried to escape from the ship; they lowered the boat into the water and pretended that they were going to put out some anchors from the front of the ship.

But Paul said to the army officer and soldiers, 'If the sailors don't stay on board, you have no hope of being saved.' So the soldiers cut the ropes that held the boat and let it go. Just before dawn, Paul begged them all to eat some food: 'You have been waiting for fourteen days now, and all this time you have not eaten anything. I beg you, then, eat some food; you need it in order to survive.

'Not even a hair of your heads will be lost.' After saying this, Paul took some bread, gave thanks to God before them all, broke it, and began to eat. They took heart, and every one of them also ate some food. There was a total of 276 of us on board. After everyone had eaten enough, they lightened the ship by throwing all the wheat into the sea.

When day came, the sailors did not recognise the coast, but they noticed a bay with a beach and decided that, if possible, they would run the ship aground there. So they cut off the anchors and let them sink in the sea, and at the same time they untied the ropes that held the steering oars.

Then they raised the sail at the front of the ship so that the wind would blow the ship forward, and we headed for shore. But the ship hit a sandbank and went aground; the front part of the ship got stuck and could not move, while the back part was being broken to pieces by the violence of the waves.

The soldiers made a plan to kill all the prisoners, in order to keep them from swimming ashore and escaping. But the army officer wanted to save Paul, so he stopped them from doing this.

Instead, he ordered those who could swim to jump overboard first and swim ashore; the rest were to follow, holding on to the planks or to some broken pieces of the ship.

And this was how we all got safely ashore.

# SHIPWRECK!

A Christian called **Paul** was being shipped across the **Mediterranean Sea** to **Rome** where he had an appointment with the **Emperor** himself.

The voyage was not going well and the ship (and all on board) had endured **fourteen days** of torment as they sailed through a **mega storm**.

That night, the sailors had a feeling that land wasn't far off and, sure enough, after dropping a line with a weight on it, they were proved right. They did the same thing a bit later and realised that the water was getting shallower. The ship was nearing land – at last!

The sailors were about to make off with the small boat but Paul stepped in and warned the Roman soldiers that *without* a crew the rest of them would all drown. So the soldiers cut the ropes and let the boat go. All for one and one for all, as they say!

As daybreak approached, Paul urged everyone to eat something so that they'd have the strength to swim ashore. Nobody had eaten a *thing* for **two whole weeks**! And no wonder. A combination of being **scared silly** and **sea sickness** was hardly gonna give them *much* of an appetite, was it?

> I BEG YOU, THEN, EAT SOME FOOD. YOU NEED IT IN ORDER TO SURVIVE. NOT EVEN A HAIR OF YOUR HEADS WILL BE LOST.

That little speech from Paul *really* encouraged them. Paul then **thanked God** (presumably for keeping them all safe) and then passed round some bread.

The ship finally came to a halt on a **sandbank** but speed was of the essence. The **pounding waves** were breaking the ship to bits moment by moment.

Just before they were about to jump ship the Roman soldiers decided that they were gonna kill all the prisoners to stop them escaping (not that they could easily escape from an island, as they soon discovered it to be) but Paul (and the Roman army officer) made sure that their plan was thwarted.

And so, clinging on to debris from the ship or swimming for all they were worth, all **276 people** on board made it ashore – just like God's angel had *promised.*

# PAUL IN MALTA

## WHAT'S IT ALL ABOUT?

This Bible story is about how Paul (and his shipmates) is washed ashore on the island of Malta plus some miraculous happenings

## WHO ARE THE MAIN CHARACTERS?

Paul, a sizzling snake, Publius and his father, and the inhabitants of Malta

## WHERE'S IT FOUND IN THE BIBLE?

Acts 28:1-10

## HERE'S THE BIBLE PASSAGE...

When we were safely ashore, we learnt that the island was called Malta.

The natives there were very friendly to us. It had started to rain and was cold, so they lit a fire and made us all welcome. Paul gathered up a bundle of sticks and was putting them on the fire when a snake came out on account of the heat and fastened itself to his hand.

The natives saw the snake hanging on Paul's hand and said to one another, 'This man must be a murderer, but Fate will not let him live, even though he escaped from the sea.'

But Paul shook the snake off into the fire without being harmed at all. They were waiting for him to swell up or suddenly fall down dead.

But after waiting for a long time and not seeing anything unusual happening to him, they changed their minds and said, 'He is a god!'

Not far from that place were some fields that belonged to Publius, the chief official of the island. He welcomed us kindly and for three days we were his guests.

Publius' father was in bed, sick with fever and dysentery.

Paul went into his room, prayed, placed his hands on him, and healed him.

When this happened, all the other sick people on the island came and were healed. They gave us many gifts, and when we sailed, they put on board what we needed for the voyage.

# SNAKES ALIVE!

The Bible story that we're *about* to check out features a world-famous Christian (well he is *now*) from way back when. His name was **Paul** and we catch up with him just as he's been washed ashore (along with his **275 shipmates**) on the **island of Malta**. Paul was being shipped to **Rome** to stand trial before the Roman Emperor – but that's *another* story.

It wasn't the *best* of days for being shipwrecked. It was **cold** and it was **wet**. Hardly a warm welcome from this Mediterranean island.

On the *plus* side, the *inhabitants* of Malta were a bit more hospitable than the grotty weather. In no time at all they'd got a **fire** going with bundles of sticks.

Being the helpful sort of chap that he was, Paul chucked a few sticks on the fire *himself*, for good measure.

At that moment a snake, that had been driven out by the **sizzling heat**, launched itself at Paul's hand. Probably none too pleased at the thought of being nearly **fried alive** – who knows?

When the Maltese people (that's what people who live in Malta are called) saw this, they put two and two together and *wrongly* assumed that Paul had done something wrong and *this* was his **come-uppance!**

THIS MAN MUST BE A MURDERER AND THOUGH HE ESCAPED FROM THE SEA HE'S NOW GETTING THE PUNISHMENT HE DESERVES!

But Paul wasn't the *least* bit bothered by what they thought, nor for that matter about the **poisonous snake**. With a flick of his arm he flung the offending snake into the fire (to finish *off* the job of getting well and truly sizzled).

Everyone waited with bated breath for Paul to keel over and drop down dead after being bitten by the snake, but they waited in vain. After what seemed like *ages*, and when Paul was *still* **very much alive**, they came to *another* wrong conclusion . . . that Paul was a god!

Fortunately for Paul (and his travelling companions) they didn't have to spend the night out in the open. **Publius** (the governor of the island) kindly put them up in his house. It must have been a big house!

Publius's *dad* was **seriously ill** so Paul went and prayed for him and, no surprises here – **he got better**. News that **God** was doing some serious stuff on the island spread like **wildfire**.

Paul had every sick person from one end of the island to the other, queuing at his door to be healed – and they all *were*. The lot of 'em.

When it was eventually time for Paul (and his entourage) to *leave* the island they didn't leave empty-handed. The islanders loaded them up with **armfuls of goodbye gifts** and lots of goodies for the voyage to Rome.

# PAUL IN ROME

## WHAT'S IT ALL ABOUT?

This Bible story is about how Paul finally reached Rome (to stand trial before the Emperor)

## WHO ARE THE MAIN CHARACTERS?

Paul, various Christians, the local Jews and last (but not least) his Roman guard

## WHERE'S IT FOUND IN THE BIBLE?

Acts 28:11-24 and 30-31

## HERE'S THE BIBLE PASSAGE...

After three months we sailed away on a ship from Alexandria, called 'The Twin Gods', which had spent the winter in the island. We arrived in the city of Syracuse and stayed there for three days. From there we sailed on and arrived in the city of Rhegium.

The next day a wind began to blow from the south, and in two days we came to the town of Puteoli. We found some believers there who asked us to stay with them a week. And so we came to Rome.

The believers in Rome heard about us and came as far as the towns of Market of Appius and Three Inns to meet us. When Paul saw them, he thanked God and was greatly encouraged. When we arrived in Rome, Paul was allowed to live by himself with a soldier guarding him.

After three days Paul called the local Jewish leaders to a meeting. When they had gathered, he said to them, 'My fellow-Israelites, even though I did nothing against our people or the customs that we received from our ancestors, I was made a prisoner in Jerusalem and handed over to the Romans. After questioning me, the Romans wanted to release me, because they found that I had done nothing for which I deserved to die. But when the Jews opposed this, I was forced to appeal to the Emperor, even though I had no accusation to make against my own people. That is why I asked to see you and talk with you.

'As a matter of fact, I am bound in chains like this for the sake of him for whom the people of Israel hope.' They said to him, 'We have not received any letters from Judea about you, nor have any of our people come from there with any news or anything bad to say about you. But we would like to hear your ideas, because we know that everywhere people speak against this party to which you belong.'

So they fixed a date with Paul, and a large number of them came that day to the place where Paul was staying. From morning till night he explained to them his message about the Kingdom of God, and he tried to convince them about Jesus by quoting from the Law of Moses and the writings of the prophets. Some of them were convinced by his words, but others would not believe.

For two years Paul lived in a place he rented for himself, and there he welcomed all who came to see him.

He preached about the Kingdom of God and taught about the Lord Jesus Christ, speaking with all boldness and freedom.

# NO PLACE LIKE ROME!

The Bible bit we're gonna look at *now* is the very **last** one you'll find in Bible book **Acts**. Paul, one of the guys who pops up *most* in this book of the Bible, had finally made it to **Rome** (in Italy).

It had been a rotten old journey, I can tell you. He'd even been in a **shipwreck** along the way, just to make matters *worse*. Anyway, that's history. The *main* thing was that Paul had made it!

Why was Paul in Rome? Simple – he'd gone there to stand trial before the **Emperor of Rome** to defend himself against a load of false accusations some **Jews** (from Jerusalem, where Paul had come from) had made *against* him.

When the local **Christians** (and some who *weren't* quite so local) found out that *Paul* was in town they dropped by to say 'hello' to this important *fellow*-Christian.

Although Paul was officially a *prisoner*, the **Romans** were pretty good about the whole thing and let him rent a place to live on his lonesome . . . with one condition.

That he had a **soldier** to guard him. I think Paul can live with that!

SO CAN I!

Once Paul had got himself settled, he sent for the local **Jews** to see if *they* had anything against him (like the Jews in *Jerusalem* had).

When Paul told 'em *who* he was and *what* he was being accused of they played dumb – they didn't know what he was talking about. In fact, they were actually quite *interested* to hear what Paul had to say about **Jesus** and the **Jewish religion**.

But when Paul *did* fill them in with the lowdown about how the Jewish religion was just the *build-up* to **Jesus**, things changed. Okay, so *some* of the Jews bought into what Paul had to say, but *others* rejected it out of hand – just like the Jews back home had done.

The Bible says that Paul lived in Rome for **two years** – and that's where the story ends. Did Paul ever get to stand before the Emperor?

Well, I think we'll have to take it as a 'yes' because when God says something's gonna happen – it does!

# ALSO AVAILABLE

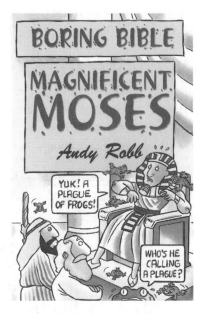

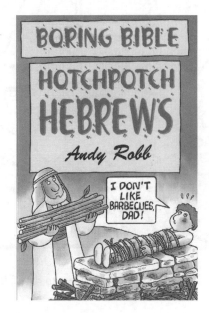

from John Hunt Publishing Ltd
46a West Street, New Alresford, Hampshire, SO24 9AU
www.johnhunt-publishing.com